T0387562

SPYWARE

by Connor Stratton

WWW.FOCUSREADERS.COM

Focus Readers is distributed by North Star Editions:
sales@northstareditions.com | 888-417-0195

Produced for Focus Readers by Red Line Editorial.

Photographs ©: Shutterstock Images, cover, 1, 4–5, 7, 8–9, 11, 14–15, 19, 20–21, 25, 27, 29; Red Line Editorial, 13; Debajyoti Chakraborty/NurPhoto/AP Images, 17; Andrzej Iwanczuk/NurPhoto/AP Images, 23

Library of Congress Cataloging-in-Publication Data
Library of Congress Cataloging-in-Publication Data is available on the Library of Congress website.

ISBN
979-8-88998-521-1 (hardcover)
979-8-88998-582-2 (ebook pdf)
979-8-88998-553-2 (hosted ebook)

Printed in the United States of America
Mankato, MN
082025

ABOUT THE AUTHOR

Connor Stratton writes and edits nonfiction children's books. He lives in Minnesota.

TABLE OF CONTENTS

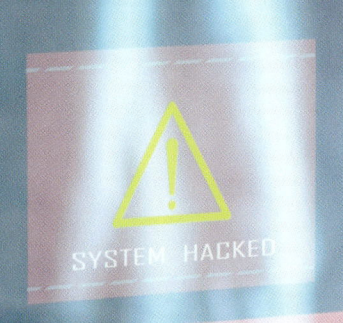

CHAPTER 1

HOTEL HACK

A man checks into a fancy hotel. He is the leader of a massive company. In his room, he opens his computer. He tries to join the hotel's Wi-Fi.

A window pops up on the man's screen. It says to update an app. The man clicks okay. He thinks he's updated the app. However, the man has just been **hacked**.

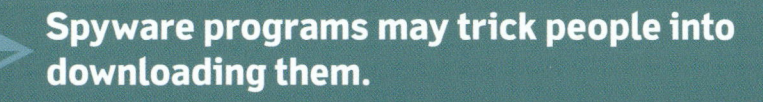

Spyware programs may trick people into downloading them.

He has downloaded spyware onto his computer. And he's completely unaware.

The spyware is known as DarkHotel. It begins tracking every action the man takes. The man logs on to his email. The spyware records his password. Then he sends a business email. The spyware records his message. Next, he searches for an important file. The spyware records exactly what he searches for.

All of this information is sent to the hackers. With it, they can learn valuable information about his company. They might learn business secrets. Or they could take his bank information. Then they could steal money.

DarkHotel hackers affected dozens of hotels around the world.

Computer researchers discovered DarkHotel in 2014. By then, the hackers had been at work for years. They hacked hotels. Then they targeted business leaders who stayed there. The hacks continued into the 2020s. They showed how dangerous spyware could be.

CHAPTER 2

HOW IT WORKS

Spyware is a type of **software**. It secretly gathers information on a computer or other device. Spyware attacks have three main steps. First, hackers need to access the target's device. Many methods involve tricking people into installing the spyware. **Phishing** is one example. Another

> Sometimes spyware can be installed on a phone with a single text message.

example is known as a Trojan. That is when hackers secretly place spyware in other software. They convince victims to download that software. For instance, someone may download a new app.

ZERO-DAY ATTACKS

Software often has **bugs**. Spyware takes advantage of bugs to hack into computers. So, software **developers** try to fix these bugs as soon as they learn about them. Users can download the fixes through updates. However, hackers sometimes find bugs before anyone else does. They start using the bugs for hacking right away. This type of hack is called a zero-day attack. It means the developer had zero days to fix it before being attacked.

Zero-click attacks are very hard to spot. A device may not show any signs of being hacked.

Without knowing, they also downloaded the spyware onto their device.

Advanced spyware may use zero-click attacks. This type of spyware can be installed on devices without the targets doing anything. That's because devices automatically check some incoming information. Zero-click attacks make use of this action. For example, a hacker may send a text or an email. The message also contains spyware. The target's device checks the message. In doing so, it downloads the spyware.

Once the spyware is installed, the second step begins. Programs spy on targets in several ways. Some spyware programs are called keyloggers. Keyloggers track what people type on their devices. The programs can learn a target's passwords. They can see what sites the person visits. Other spyware tracks people's locations. Still others turn on microphones and cameras. The spyware records what those tools pick up.

In the third step, the spyware sends all this **data** to the hacker. The hacker can use it for a variety of purposes.

APPS SPYWARE CAN ACCESS

finance apps

social media

messaging services

maps

photos

camera

CHAPTER 3

PURPOSE AND IMPACT

Spyware has many purposes. Some uses are legal. For example, some police groups use spyware. They use programs to gather evidence of crimes. That helps them catch suspects.

Countries use spyware during wars. Leaders often want to know the plans of their enemies. So, some countries use

Some parents use apps to monitor what their kids see online. They may explain that it helps keep the kids safe.

spyware to gather information. Then, they can gain an advantage in the conflict.

However, many governments use spyware for other reasons, too. Leaders may want to protect their power. But journalists and **activists** might speak out against the leaders. Or politicians with different opinions may try to win elections against them. Leaders may view these people as threats. So, some leaders use spyware on them. They gather information and try to stop their opponents.

Using spyware in this way can be harmful. For example, **democracies** rely on voters having information. That way,

In 2022, people in India protested against the country's ruling party. They opposed the government's use of a spyware program called Pegasus.

voters can make decisions in a way that matches their values. Journalists and activists play key roles in informing the public. But if spyware stops those people, democracies can become weaker.

Individuals use spyware for harmful reasons as well. For instance, people in unhealthy relationships may use it. Some people install spyware on their partners' phones. Then they can track their partners' every move. The targeted partners often feel controlled and unsafe.

ADWARE

One type of software is called adware. It works similarly to spyware. Companies place it in apps. The adware tracks what people buy or search for. Then companies use that data. They show users ads that relate to their interests. Those people may be more likely to buy the companies' products. However, people can sometimes make choices about adware. They can allow or block adware on their devices. This makes it different from spyware.

Spyware victims can sometimes get back the money they lost. But it is not always possible.

People also use spyware for **identity theft**. Hackers steal financial information, such as banking passwords. Then they log in to victims' bank accounts. Hackers may buy expensive things. Victims can lose large amounts of money.

CHAPTER 4

SPYWARE SOLUTIONS

Spyware is different from some other cyber threats. That's because many companies make and sell spyware legally. However, people can use legal spyware for harmful goals. For this reason, some groups argue that all spyware should be banned. Others believe spyware can be useful. They do not want to ban it.

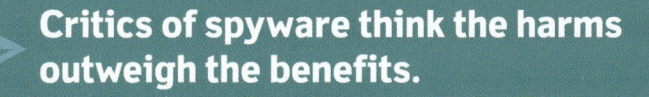

Critics of spyware think the harms outweigh the benefits.

However, they argue that spyware needs stronger rules.

Spyware companies can be more careful with how their programs are used. They can take action if programs are used in harmful ways. For example, one company sold spyware to the Serbian government. In 2024, a group showed that Serbia was using that spyware against activists and reporters. In 2025, the company took action. Leaders said it would stop doing business with Serbia.

Some companies aren't making these changes. That's where governments come in. Leaders can pass new laws making rules about spyware. And they can make

In 2024, leaders in Poland were investigated for illegally using a spyware program.

new laws about people who use spyware in harmful ways.

Governments can also crack down on harmful companies. That happened in the United States in 2021. That year, the US government banned government agencies from working with some spyware companies.

Other tech companies can help stop harmful spyware, too. For example, tech companies can improve their own cybersecurity. They can fix bugs faster. That way, it's harder for spyware to gain access. Companies can introduce new programs as well. In 2022, Apple released Lockdown Mode. This setting was meant for people at risk of spyware attacks. That included journalists and activists. Lockdown Mode alerted people to powerful spyware attacks. The program was successful. It showed that better cybersecurity was possible.

People can download apps that help look for spyware.

However, spyware is always changing. Hackers often make new programs. So, current protection software may have trouble finding it. For this reason, people keep working on better protection programs. Some programs try to spot the spyware. They look for known spyware software. Others look for patterns that are common to spyware instead. Researchers also track new spyware and new bugs. They let people know about ways to stay protected.

CITIZEN LAB

Citizen Lab formed in 2001. The group researches many topics, including cybersecurity. In the 2010s, Citizen Lab brought attention to Pegasus. This spyware can show hackers every text, photo, and video on a phone. It can track locations and record with microphones and cameras. Pegasus was supposed to help law enforcement. But many governments were using it for harmful reasons. Citizen Lab showed the world its dangers. But the group also showed how people could protect themselves.

Some companies hold trainings about how to keep devices safe from spyware.

Education is part of blocking spyware, too. People can learn about how spyware works. They can also learn ways to stop spyware from getting on their devices. That way, people can play a key role in keeping their information safe.

SPYWARE PROTECTION

People can take steps to protect against spyware. First, they should keep their devices up to date. Those updates can fix bugs. That way, spyware can't take advantage of the bugs. People should use recent antivirus software, too. Antivirus software can spot many spyware programs. Then the spyware can be removed.

People should make thoughtful choices on their devices. For example, kids should not download apps without checking with an adult. Also, people should avoid clicking on any links without looking at them carefully. These steps help stop spyware from reaching devices in the first place.

People can also change some app settings to protect against spyware. Apps such as video

People should check for available updates on computers, phones, and other devices.

chat services need access to microphones and cameras. But many other programs do not need this access. People can change their settings to not allow it. By making these privacy choices, people can help protect their information.

FOCUS QUESTIONS

Write your answers on a separate piece of paper.

1. Write a paragraph explaining the main ideas of Chapter 4.

2. Do you think all spyware should be banned? Why or why not?

3. When did Apple release Lockdown Mode?

- **A.** 2001
- **B.** 2014
- **C.** 2022

4. What is the final step of a spyware attack?

- **A.** gaining access to a device
- **B.** gathering information on the device
- **C.** sending information to the hacker

Answer key on page 32.

GLOSSARY

activists
People who take action to make social or political changes.

bugs
Problems or mistakes in software.

data
Information collected to study or track something.

democracies
Systems of government in which the people have power. Democracies typically involve elections.

developers
People who make and design software.

hacked
Had another person illegally gain access to one's device, account, or information.

identity theft
The act of stealing people's personal information, such as credit card numbers.

phishing
A cyberattack that uses a message to trick a victim into giving up personal information.

software
Programs that run on a computer and perform certain functions.

TO LEARN MORE

BOOKS

Carser, A. R. *Protect Your Data and Identity Online.* BrightPoint Press, 2022.

London, Martha. *Cybersecurity.* Bearport Publishing, 2023.

Spanier, Kristine, MLIS. *Digital Footprint.* Jump!, 2025.

NOTE TO EDUCATORS

Visit **www.focusreaders.com** to find lesson plans, activities, links, and other resources related to this title.

INDEX